CONVERSATIONS WITH MY CAT

Chuck McKenzie & MacReady McKenzie

With Ripley McKenzie

www.daftnotions.com

First published by Daft Notions in 2023

Daft Notions www.daftnotions.com

Melbourne, Victoria, Australia

Copyright © Chuck McKenzie and MacReady McKenzie

All rights reserved. No part of this book may be reproduced or transmitted in any form or by any means, including Internet search engines and retailers, electronic or mechanical, photocopying (except under the provisions of the Australian Copyright Act 1968), recording or by any information storage and retrieval system, without prior permission by the publisher.

National Library of Australia Cataloguing-in-Publication data.

CONVERSATIONS WITH MY CAT

ISBN: 978-0-6458945-0-9 (paperback)

ISBN: 978-0-6458945-1-6 (ebook)

Cover Design, Proofreading & Copy-Editing © All In The Edit

www.allintheedit.com

Editorial Management, Design, Typesetting, Publication, Coffee and Supervision of Idiots by Ripley McKenzie

Printed by IngramSpark

Spelling in this book is standard Australian, which is better value for money as readers get more vowels than they would with U.S. spelling.

Humour, Pets, Philosophy

Dedication

Chuck

To mum and dad, both of whom encouraged and supported me in everything I ever did, no matter how batshit-crazy some of those things may have seemed. I'd also like to thank all my friends for being there through good times, bad times, hangovers, relationship fails, sci-fi conventions, nightclub culture, bookshops, and cat-related silliness. Extra-special thanks to my kids, for not reporting me to Child Services on account of my Dad Jokes. And to Sarah, for love, support and laughter.

And of course huge thanks to MacReady: friend, foil, royal pain-in-the-arse, and provider of raw content. Love you, buddy!

MacReady

I'd like to thank all those without whom this book could not have been written. So I'd like to thank myself.

Oh, and I'd like to thank my accountant for pointing out that I could claim my litter tray as a tax deduction because I do my business there.

Ripley

I'd like to acknowledge the pointlessness of existence in an increasingly cold and uncaring Universe; that infinite yawning void, wherein a few fragile specks of life teeter briefly and futilely at the edge of extinction before inevitably plunging into oblivion, forever wiped from history and memory alike.

What random people said about *Conversations With My Cat*

'An hilarious romp as man pits his intellect against moggies. Can you guess who's going to win?'
Edwina Harvey, author of *The Whale's Tale*

'This book proves I'm not crazy, regardless of what my cats say.'
Ruby Daggers, Social Media Manager for *Fred The Dead Skellyman*

'This book puts the "cat" in "scatological".'
Keith Stevenson, author of *Traitor's Run*

'*Conversations With My Cat* is like *Garfield* for adults.'
Keira McKenzie, adoptive mother to Baba Yaga (cat)

'In the end times, a dark lord will rise. The last of humanity will fear and venerate him as they huddle around their pitiful fires, waiting for the rising seas to consume their last hope. His name is MacReady. This book shall be his gospel.'
Jason Franks, writer of *The Sixsmiths*

'I laughed so hard I nearly wet my pants.'
Holly Delight-Me, Burlesque Performer

'Easy to read and highly amusing – but please stop making me laugh when I'm coughing up my lungs from Covid!'
Suzie, Bookstagrammer at *suzsspace*

'A great book that makes me want to smoke some hard catnip and run for the litter tray. I give it 5 furballs out of 5.'
Daniel Palo, author of *Knock Knock Jokes From a Daggy Dad*

'Cats! It's lucky for them that we love them...troublesome little beasties...'
Damien Saunders, Cat Owner

'It's always sad when an animal is cleverer than its owner. Even sadder when the owner thinks he can write a book about it. But here we are, and here we have *Conversations With My Cat*...'
Stephen Ormsby, author of *The Whisperer and the Wanderer*

'You were such a lovely boy when you were growing up. When did you start talking to cats?'
J. A. McKenzie, co-editor of *The Worlds Contracted Thus*, **and Chuck's mum**

What random people said about 'Roget's Thesaurus'

'It's okay.'
Arthur Nonce (retired) from No.42.

The New Addition

Chuck: Hey, Miss Ripley!

Ripley: Mm.

Chuck: So you remember we were talking about getting another cat?

Ripley: No.

Chuck: I mean...we definitely were. About a month ago.

Ripley: I recall you saying, 'Wouldn't it be nice to get another cat?'

Chuck: Yeah, and you agreed.

Ripley: I believe my exact words were, 'Mm-hm'.

Chuck: That wasn't an agreement?

Ripley: It was me not getting involved in a discussion, is what it was.

Chuck: Ah.

Ripley: Is there a particular reason you're bringing this up now? And does it, perchance, have anything to do with that large box you came in with?

Chuck: Well –

Ripley: It's a rhetorical question. You clearly went out and got another cat.

Chuck: Are you…upset?

Ripley: I'm completely ambivalent.

Chuck: Oh. Good…?

Ripley: But we should probably get a few ground rules sorted before you inflict it –

Chuck: Him.

Ripley: – before you inflict *him* upon this household and its occupants.

Chuck: Sounds reasonable. So…?

Ripley: Well, first off, separate food bowls.

Chuck: Sorted.

Ripley: And separate litter trays.

Chuck: Oh, absolutely. The current one is scarcely big enough to deal with *your* output.

Ripley: Meaning what, exactly?

Chuck: Meaning that, given the frankly impossible volume of poop that comes out of such a small cat, I sometimes suspect you're actually a TARDIS.

Ripley: Rude. And I want separate houses.

Chuck: Right. So, you *are* upset.

Ripley: I'm not upset. I'm just very disappointed.

Chuck: Look, I just thought that you'd appreciate another cat to keep you company.

Ripley: Have I ever given you the slightest indication that I crave any company other than my own?

Chuck: It seems rude to answer that.

Ripley: I mean, I barely tolerate *you*.

Chuck: Hey!

Ripley: So. This new cat.

Chuck: Look, come and meet him. I'm sure you'll get along fantastically.

...

Chuck: Reasonably confident.

...

Chuck: Stop giving me that look.

Ripley: That's my regular everyday 'dealing with you' look.

Chuck: I don't like it.

Ripley: Well, I don't like that you got another cat. So.

Chuck: Come and meet him. He's lovely. I've called him 'MacReady', and he's a ginger kitten and he's sooooo cute, full of energy and fun.

Ripley: I hate him already.

Chuck: Stop that. Look, he's just young and inexperienced in...cat stuff, so I'm relying upon you to sort of...train him up. Show him the ropes. Teach him how to Cat.

Ripley: Huh.

Chuck: What?

Ripley: Well, it's just that I never considered that angle to having to cohabit with another cat.

Chuck: And?

Ripley: I mean, teaching a kitten everything I know. Instructing them on how to make their way in the world. Moulding them. Creating a tiny replica of myself, compliant to my will...

Chuck: Well –

Ripley: That would make me...sort of like a God, wouldn't it?

Chuck: I... Look, let's meet the kitten, okay?

Ripley: Fine.

Chuck: I'll just open the box up. Be gentle and quiet, though, okay? He's very little and shy and probably a bit scared.

Ripley: And yours is the first face he'll see when we open the box? You monster.

Chuck: I mean it. Be nice. And quiet. And restrained.

Ripley: Just open the box.

Chuck: Okay. So, quietly and gently, let's open...up...the box, and –

MacReady: *WASSUPP MOTHERFUCKEEEEEEEERS!!!*

...

MacReady: Too much?

Ripley: Right, I'm off to scowl in a corner.

Chuck: It strikes me that this little family setup could be the perfect basis for a book...

Ripley: Well, you can leave me out of it.

Chuck: But –

Ripley: Consider my scowl an example of foreshadowing.

Chuck: Okay, fine. I'll make this bit the last bit you're in. Probably.

Setting the Tone

MacReady: Hey! Watcha doing?

Chuck: Writing.

MacReady: Oh. Okay.

Chuck: Except that you have your paw on the keyboard.

MacReady: Yes?

Chuck: Well, I can't get to the 'A'.

MacReady: Yeah. Yeah, that's unfortunate.

Chuck: Well, could you move your paw?

MacReady: I mean, I *could*.

...

Chuck: You haven't moved your paw.

MacReady: Conserving my strength.

Chuck: Look, this is important –

MacReady: What are you writing?

Chuck: A book. It's all about –

MacReady: Sorry, I lost interest after I stopped talking. Feed me?

Chuck: Fed you already.

MacReady: Feed me again.

Chuck: No.

MacReady: Feed me?

Chuck: No!

MacReady: Look how cute I am.

Chuck: Writing. Move your paw. Go away.

MacReady: Want me to shit in your shoes?

Chuck: *WHAT?*

MacReady: I said, 'Why is this writing important?'

Chuck: Because I want to finish this book so I can sell it.

MacReady: So, you'll make a lot of money if you sell it? And you can buy lots of cat food?

Chuck: Um.

MacReady: In other words, 'No'?

Chuck: Well...

MacReady: I fail to see how this benefits me.

Chuck: It benefits *me*.

...

MacReady: I don't understand.

Chuck: Please move your paw?

MacReady: Your time really would be better spent if you went to work and earned decent cat food money instead of sitting here writing.

Chuck: Listen, I've just spent the past month unemployed, mooching around the house and lavishing you with attention. Last week I finally got a job, had one shift, and you threw a conniption fit because I wasn't home all day.

MacReady: Yes. And your point is?

Chuck: You want me to go out and slave for cat food, but you don't want me to leave the house?

MacReady: Yeah. That's about the size of it.

Chuck: I can't do both. You're being an arse.

MacReady: Hey, don't get pissy at me just because *you* can't multitask.

Chuck: Look, if I pat you and feed you now, will you let me write?

MacReady: No. The moment's passed. Tired now. I'll just lie down here.

...

MacReady: You weren't using this keyboard, were you?

Chuck: *ARRGH!!!*

MacReady: Didn't think so. No point using a keyboard if you can't get to the 'A'.

Antisocial Media

MacReady: Watcha doing?

Chuck: Looking at videos on TikTok. Heh-heh-heh!

MacReady: Funny?

Chuck: Yeah, funny cat videos.

MacReady: Funny cats?

Chuck: Y'know – cats doing silly stuff, acting like idiots, jumping around like ninjas. That sort of thing.

MacReady: So...funnier than me?

Chuck: Aw, jeez...

MacReady: Am I not enough for you?

Chuck: Look, it's just a compilation of cats doing...funny stuff. That's all. It's funny.

MacReady: You used to think *I* was funny. And cute.

Chuck: Still do. But this is like...

MacReady: Other cats.

Chuck: Yeah. I mean, no. Look, it's all the funny bits in a ten-minute video, without all the boring bits.

MacReady: Boring bits? So, now I'm boring? When I'm not being funny or cute I'm boring?

Chuck: I didn't say that.

MacReady: That's okay. By all means look at other cats if that's what you need to do. Just so long as you understand that real cats aren't funny all of the time like they are in these videos.

Chuck: All right! I'm sorry if I hurt your feelings.

MacReady: Hmph.

Chuck: You're an awesome cat. Very cute, very funny.

MacReady: You're just saying that.

Chuck: No, honestly!

MacReady: Well... Okay, then.

Chuck: Okay.

MacReady: If you like...

Chuck: What?

MacReady: Well, I could be funny for you now. You could watch *me* being funny. I can still be funny, you know.

Chuck: Um... Okay. Yeah. Sure. Why not.

MacReady: Okay, cool. Right, here we go...

...

Chuck: You're...not doing anything.

MacReady: You have to wait for it.

Chuck: You are literally not doing anything except lying across the laptop keyboard.

MacReady: I'm being ironically funny.

Chuck: You're an arse.

MacReady: I'm being arthouse.

Chuck: I'm outta here.

MacReady: I'll just stay here and watch videos of attentive and responsible cat-owners, shall I?

Location, Location, Location

MacReady: Hey!

Chuck: *BUH!*

MacReady: Not the reaction I was expecting.

Chuck: What are you doing in the sock drawer?

MacReady: I'm...not doing *anything* in the sock drawer. What are you implying?

Chuck: No, I mean, why are you *in* the sock drawer?

MacReady: Oh. Well, the underwear drawer was full.

Chuck: Yes.

MacReady: With underwear.

Chuck: Yes. As it should be.

MacReady: Oh. Really?

Chuck: Yeah. That's the primary function of the underwear drawer.

MacReady: Is it?

Chuck: Yeah. Hence the description 'underwear drawer'.

MacReady: Huh. Well, there you go, then. You learn something new every day.

Chuck: You really didn't know that?

MacReady: Well, no. I'd always assumed the underwear drawer was for my early-morning nap. Today it was over-filled, so I had to resort to the secondary napping drawer.

Chuck: The sock drawer.

MacReady: The – as you say – sock drawer.

Chuck: The sock drawer is for socks.

MacReady: Okay, now you're just freaking me out.

Chuck: Hang on – do you actually think that everything in this house is there solely for the purpose of your comfort?

MacReady: You have that look on your face. You're about to tell me I'm wrong, aren't you?

Chuck: You're a genius.

MacReady: Jeez, why don't you have done with it and tell your kids Santa doesn't exist?

Chuck: So, what did you think, say, the bed was for?

MacReady: My night-time naps. I actually thought I was being magnanimous in allowing you to share it.

Chuck: The washing machine?

MacReady: Naps.

Chuck: Laundry basket?

MacReady: Naps.

Chuck: The chair in my study?

MacReady: Sharpening my claws on – I mean, naps...?

Chuck: Okay, look, I don't have an issue with you napping on stuff. Just keep in mind that none of it is actually *yours*, so can you please treat it with respect?

MacReady: S'pose.

Chuck: And no clawing the chair in my study.

MacReady: Okay.

Chuck: Okay. Well, I'm glad we had this talk. Which reminds me, I need to empty the litter tray.

MacReady: Yeah, good idea. It must be getting dusty.

Chuck: You mean smelly.

MacReady: No. Dusty. Because you hardly ever rake it.

Chuck: Rake it?

MacReady: Yes. I mean, that's what you do with a Zen Garden, isn't it?

Chuck: It's...not a Zen Garden.

MacReady: Oh. Then what's it for?

Chuck: It's...for you to crap in.

...

MacReady: Whut?

Chuck: You...didn't know that?

MacReady: You have that look on your face again.

Chuck: So, where the hell have you been crapping all this time??

MacReady: Here and there.

Chuck: Meaning?

MacReady: Meaning, you may not want to look in your shirt drawer.

An Exercise in Solipsism. Or Something.

MacReady: You weren't here today.

Chuck: No.

MacReady: You were somewhere else.

Chuck: Yes. That's why I wasn't here.

MacReady: But I needed you here.

Chuck: I had to be somewhere else.

MacReady: This feels like a circular argument.

Chuck: I had to work.

MacReady: But you worked last week.

Chuck: Yes...?

...

Chuck: Okay. You do understand that work is an ongoing thing, don't you? I have to go to work *five days a week* in order to keep getting paid money to live on.

MacReady: And buy cat food.

Chuck: And buy cat food.

MacReady: Well, that's just dumb. It needs to stop.

Chuck: I can't stop working. If I did that I'd have no money to live on.

MacReady: Or to buy cat food.

Chuck: Or to buy cat food.

MacReady: Well, you need to organise someone to pay you to stay home with me.

Chuck: And do nothing?

MacReady: Well, only when I don't need you.

Chuck: Nobody gets paid to do nothing.

MacReady: What about those Real Housewives of Beverley Hills?

Chuck: Look, what did you need me for today, anyway?

MacReady: I needed you to play with me. To run up and down the stairs. To wave around that fluffy thing-on-a-stick. To tickle my tummy while I lacerate your hands.

Chuck: Right. Well, while I was unemployed I spent many a day at home with you, which gave me the opportunity to observe your routines.

MacReady: Okay.

Chuck: So, I feel I may already know the answer to the following question, but will ask regardless.

MacReady: Fire away.

Chuck: About how long would this proposed 'play session' you've cited have lasted?

MacReady: About five minutes.

Chuck: Right.

MacReady: Well, it takes a great deal out of you, play. Need to nap beforehand, nap afterwards...

Chuck: So — and do please correct me if I'm misrepresenting you here — you feel I should stay home at all times, thereby sacrificing my current employment and with it any expectations of an ongoing salary in order to make myself available for the — at best — five minutes of the day when you decide you need me to play with you?

MacReady: Look at you! And people say you're the stupid one in this relationship.

...

MacReady: I mean, you *are*, but —

Chuck: What people?

MacReady: Smart people.

...

MacReady: You don't know them.

Chuck: Okay, well, me staying home to play with you is not going to happen.

MacReady: How dare you.

Chuck: You'll just have to rearrange your schedule and reserve play for when I get home.

MacReady: Do you have any idea how much effort goes into organising a daily schedule?

Chuck: No.

MacReady: I shall tell you.

Chuck: Please don't.

MacReady: Nap. Food. Nap. Toilet break. Food. Nap. Play. Nap, food, pee, nap, snooze, sleep, big sleep, night-time sleep, and – if time permits – a quick session of batshit-crazy zoomies at two in the morning.

Chuck: Right.

MacReady: All meticulously planned. All precisely timed. So you going to work right in the middle of my morning nap then barging back through the door in the middle of my afternoon pee break has the potential to throw my schedule completely out of whack. And then we have chaos. So you'll have to stay home.

Chuck: You are such a selfish arse.

MacReady: Hey, do I come to *your* work and tell you how to do your job?

Knowledge is Pain

Chuck: We need to talk.

MacReady: Oo. Sounds serious.

Chuck: It is.

MacReady: Okay, allow me to adopt my 'serious discussion' pose.

Chuck: Your 'serious discussion' pose is identical to your 'I don't give a shit' pose.

MacReady: Your powers of observation virtually qualify as a superpower.

Chuck: Okay, listen. Remember I had to explain to you recently that the litter tray is, in fact, there for you to crap in?

MacReady: I do remember that, as it happens.

Chuck: As opposed to you crapping in my shirt drawer.

MacReady: Fun times.

Chuck: I checked your litter tray today.

MacReady: Okay.

...

MacReady: This wasn't much of a talk, really, was it?

Chuck: I was waiting to see if there was anything you wanted to tell me.

MacReady: Such as?

Chuck: Regarding the litter tray?

MacReady: I'm really not great with this sort of passive-aggressive questioning. Could you be more specific?

Chuck: There was no crap in your litter tray.

MacReady: Excellent. No need to clean it, right?

Chuck: A more pressing concern of mine is where you are currently crapping.

MacReady: Oh. That would be in the litter tray.

Chuck: You can't be using the litter tray.

MacReady: I am.

Chuck: But you can't be.

MacReady: But I am.

Chuck: No, no, no.

MacReady: Yes, yes, yes.

Chuck: Listen – there is no crap in your litter tray.

MacReady: Correct.

Chuck: And you want me to believe that you're not crapping elsewhere?

MacReady: I'd certainly appreciate that.

Chuck: So, if you *are* using the litter tray, then where the hell is the crap disappearing to?

MacReady: Ah.

Chuck: What?

MacReady: I'm suddenly sensing that you may not like my answer.

Chuck: Oh, I'm counting on it. But I still want to know.

MacReady: Promise not to yell at me?

Chuck: No.

MacReady: How about if I break it to you gently?

Chuck: Whatever. Give it up.

MacReady: Okay, let me put it like this...

...

Chuck: You're not saying anything.

MacReady: I'm doing my impersonation of Conservative politicians addressing allegations of corruption within the party.

Chuck: Oh for –

MacReady: Political and edgy. That's me.

Chuck: WHERE IS THE CRAP DISAPPEARING TO, YOU PAIN-IN-THE-ARSE CAT??

MacReady: Okay, look, you know how we occasionally look after your girlfriend's dog when she has to go away for work?

Chuck: Yes?

MacReady: Well, if I were you, I'd stop letting the dog lick you on the mouth.

...

Chuck: I'm going to the bathroom. I may be some time.

MacReady: Good idea. Mouthwash will help.

Can't Live With Them,

Can't Bury Them in a Shallow Grave

MacReady: Hey! Feed me?

Chuck: Already did.

MacReady: Feed me!

Chuck: Already did!

MacReady: Did you?

Chuck: I did.

MacReady: Huh.

...

MacReady: Feed me?

Chuck: ALREADY DID!

MacReady: Oh.

...

MacReady: Where did you put the food?

Chuck: In your food bowl.

MacReady: Oh.

Chuck: Where else?

MacReady: Mrow?

Chuck: What?

MacReady: Feed me?

Chuck: I – seriously? I literally just told you that I put food in your food bowl already!!

MacReady: Did you?

Chuck: Yes!

MacReady: Definitely?

Chuck: Yes!

MacReady: You definitely heard yourself say it?

Chuck: Yes! I was actually here when I said it! I heard the whole thing!

MacReady: Huh. Okay.

Chuck: So, go eat!

MacReady: I will.

...

Chuck: I swear, if you ask me to feed you one more time I will lose my shit.

MacReady: I'm hungry.

Chuck: Listen, you stupid moggy – I HAVE FED YOU ALREADY! THE FOOD IS IN YOUR BOWL!

MacReady: Right.

Chuck: Okay??

MacReady: Okay.

Chuck: Good!

MacReady: And my bowl is where?

Chuck: OVER THERE!

MacReady: Can you show me?

Chuck: Oh for – *there!* Happy?

MacReady: Where's the food?

Chuck: There!

MacReady: Where?

Chuck: *THERE!*

MacReady: Not seeing it.

Chuck: See how my index finger is sunk up to the knuckle in brown goop?

MacReady: Move your hand... Okay. Yeah.

Chuck: The brown goop is the food.

MacReady: Huh.

Chuck: Well? Are you going to eat it?

MacReady: Eat what?

Chuck: Seriously, I am this close to shoving my hand up your arse and using you as an oven mitt.

MacReady: Oh! You mean this food here?

...

MacReady: Yeah. You're talking about this food here.

...

MacReady: Stop looking at me like that.

...

MacReady: I can't eat under this sort of pressure.

Chuck: What the hell is it with you and food? In fact, what the hell is it with every cat I've ever known and food? It's like the food is bloody invisible! Do you know how many times we've been through this bloody routine in just the last week? FOUR! Four bloody times! It drives me crazy and it's like it just never sinks in! I mean, how hard is it to just listen and register that the food has been placed in your bowl without all of this douchebaggery? ARRGH!

MacReady: Gotta make my own fun.

Chuck: What was that?

MacReady: I said, 'Sorry, it won't happen again.'

Chuck: Really?

MacReady: Really.

Chuck: Promise?

MacReady: Promise.

Chuck: Well, okay then. I need to cool down. I'm just gonna go back to my chair and get back to what I was doing before you demented me, which was reading my book.

MacReady: Same time tomorrow, sucker...

Chuck: Eh?

MacReady: Meow. Omnomnomnomnom...

Consequences, Be'atch

MacReady: I love you!

Chuck: N'awwww!

MacReady: Let me cuddle up against you and stretch my paws up to touch your face!

Chuck: Cute!

MacReady: I just buried my shit with these paws. Next time you buy the wrong tinned food I'll be rubbing them on your lips as you sleep.

Privileges of Opposable Thumbs

MacReady: Hey! Are you eating bacon??

Chuck: No...?

...

MacReady: You know I'm gonna go shit in your shoes now, right?

Chuck: MY bacon!

Music Doth Soothe the Savage Beast

MacReady: Watcha doing?

Chuck: Listening to music on my phone.

MacReady: I'm hearing nothing. Is this a 'voices-in-my-head' kinda thing?

Chuck: I'm using earphones.

MacReady: Ah. And that enhances the experience, does it?

Chuck: Earphones let me listen to the music without bothering anyone else.

MacReady: Well, it bothers *me* that you're wearing them, so they're not working too well, are they?

Chuck: Why would it bother you that I'm wearing them?

MacReady: I chew on them when you're not here. It's pretty off-putting that they've been in your ears. Though it does explain the flavour.

...

MacReady: You have that look on your face.

Chuck: Go away.

MacReady: What sort of music are you listening to?

Chuck: I can pull the earphones out so you can hear if you like?

MacReady: Okay.

...

MacReady: What in the Name of Bast is that?

Chuck: 'Barbie Girl' by Aqua.

MacReady: Is that one of the tracks your girlfriend insists you play only when she's not in the house?

Chuck: Well...

MacReady: One of the many, many tracks?

Chuck: We just have different tastes.

MacReady: Obviously. She likes music, you like noise pollution.

Chuck: Oi!

MacReady: Sorry. I'm sure that track is considered a cultural masterpiece among...you people.

...

MacReady: Not being racist.

Chuck: It's just that she's not specifically into nineties music. So I don't play it when she's home.

MacReady: If you could extend the same courtesy to me, I'd greatly appreciate it.

Chuck: Cheeky shit. What does a cat know about good music, anyway?

MacReady: More than you, apparently.

Chuck: No, come on, illuminate me as to the rich cultural heritage of cat music.

MacReady: All cats have a natural appreciation of music.

Chuck: Okay.

MacReady: We're born with it, like the instinct to hunt. Or to piss on suede shoes. And we're all astoundingly talented singers.

Chuck: I'm unconvinced.

MacReady: Then prepare to be convinced!

Chuck: This must be how Oppenheimer felt.

MacReady: Want me to sing something for you?

Chuck: Okay, sure, I guess – OH DEAR GOD THAT NOISE PLEASE GOD MAKE IT STOP what the HELL was that??

MacReady: That, my friend, was the Song of My People.

Chuck: Bloody hell! Sounded more like – uh...

MacReady: If you say, 'Two cats screwing', I will be extremely offended.

Chuck: I, ah...wasn't...

MacReady: You can't say that. Only *we* can say that.

Chuck: Look, if I promise to keep my earphones on when listening to music, will you promise to not sing?

MacReady: I dunno. Sometimes a cat's just gotta sing. Heart full of joy and all that.

Chuck: There's half a bag of fresh catnip in it for you.

MacReady: You can do better than that.

Chuck: Full bag if you let me listen to my music with the earphones off sometimes.

MacReady: Hm. What sort of music, specifically?

Chuck: I don't know. Is there anything in my music library to which you don't object?

MacReady: Let me think...

...

Chuck: Oh, come on!

MacReady: Shh. Thinking.

Chuck: You're being an arse is what you're doing.

MacReady: Actually, there is one thing of yours I don't mind.

Chuck: Just one?

MacReady: Take the win. If you have other stuff that sounds like this one thing, we can extend the exemption.

Chuck: Okay. Shoot.

MacReady: Remember last Wednesday?

Chuck: Um...

MacReady: You were at home. Moving all of those boxes from the kitchen to the garage

Chuck: Oh, jeez, the day I fell downstairs, you mean?

MacReady: And lay there with half a tonne of busted crockery all over you, begging and moaning.

Chuck: Don't remind me! But what music was I playing that day? I don't even...

...

Chuck: You are such an arse.

MacReady: A beautiful soundscape of broken souls.

Chuck: I really, really hate you.

MacReady: Know any more like that one?

Hurdy-Gurdy Cat

Ripley: Hey!!!

Chuck: Hey?

Ripley: Oh my God. It's full of stars!

Chuck: 'Scuse me?

Ripley: Look at me, I'm Parliamentary Question Time! DURR! DURR! DURR!

Chuck: What?

Ripley: I'm a dragon. HA-HA-HA-HA-HA!

Chuck: I take it you found the catnip stash.

Ripley: Medicinal user, man.

An Examination of the Impact of Opposable Thumbs Upon the Development of Human Civilisation. And Stuff.

MacReady: Watcha doing?

Chuck: Just going through the bookshelf, checking out some books I haven't read in a while.

MacReady: Sounds fabulous.

Chuck: Absolutely.

MacReady: No, wait – what's that other term? Tedious. That's it.

Chuck: Not at all. Check out this cool book on the history of civilisation!

MacReady: Human civilisation?

Chuck: Yeah...?

MacReady: Okay.

Chuck: What?

MacReady: Nothing. It's cute that this stuff gets you so enthused.

Chuck: Why wouldn't it?

MacReady: I dunno. A working sense of perspective, perhaps?

Chuck: What are you talking about? Look at this amazing stuff! Ancient Mesopotamia, the cradle of civilisation!

MacReady: Pfft!

Chuck: What?

MacReady: Wouldn't have been worth crap if cats hadn't kept the crops free from pests.

Chuck: Um, no, Mesopotamia predated Ancient Egypt.

MacReady: Right. And?

Chuck: And the Ancient Egyptians were the first to domesticate cats.

MacReady: I question the term 'domesticate'. And you are incorrect.

Chuck: Nope. Well-known fact.

MacReady: Noted in that book, huh?

Chuck: Yup.

MacReady: And this book was published…when?

Chuck: Let's see…1972.

MacReady: Mm-hm. Care to Google it? Just on the off-chance that new knowledge has been added to the shallow pool of human wisdom sometime over the past fifty-odd years?

Chuck: Okay smartarse...let's see...

...

Chuck: Ah.

MacReady: And in breaking news, the world isn't flat either.

Chuck: How did you know about Mesopotamia?

MacReady: We cats have an extensive race-memory, instantly accessible, that puts your puny human Internet to shame.

...

MacReady: Okay, I saw it on The History Channel.

Chuck: Okay. Don't gloat.

MacReady: Don't knock my hobbies.

Chuck: Okay, well...moving on, check out this architecture from Ancient Greece!

MacReady: Cats. Crops.

...

MacReady: You're looking at the page on Ancient Egypt now, aren't you?

Chuck: No...

...

Chuck: Yes.

MacReady: 'Nuff said. Human civilisation would be utterly crap without cats.

Chuck: Look, I'll concede that cats clearly helped to *shape* human civilisation, but it's not like they actually *built* any of this stuff. The Parthenon! The Pyramids! The Big Prawn!

MacReady: True. But we could have.

Chuck: Riiiiight...

MacReady: We just never needed to.

Chuck: You are so full of crap. And I can give you at least one definitive reason why cats could never have built a civilisation, which is that you can't manipulate tools without opposable thumbs. Thus, cats can't build stuff. Q.E.D.

MacReady: You're ugly when you're smug. And at all other times. And do you even know what Q.E.D means?

Chuck: Of course. It means, 'In your face'. Now, bask in my physiological superiority, feline!

MacReady: I should pity you. And yet, I shall delight in shattering your world view.

Chuck: What do you mean?

MacReady: Come into the kitchen.

Chuck: Um...okay.

MacReady: Grab a can of cat food. And the tin-opener. That's it...

Chuck: And this is going to prove you don't need opposable thumbs...how?

MacReady: Just watch and learn. Now, very slowly, open the can.

Chuck: Okay...

MacReady: And take note of *exactly* what's going on as you do it.

Chuck: Well, I'm using my opposable thumbs, for one thing.

MacReady: Shh. Just concentrate. Are you concentrating?

Chuck: Yes. But I still don't see –

MacReady: You'll get it in a moment, I guarantee.

Chuck: Okay. Can's open. Where's my epiphany?

MacReady: Almost there. Now, put the food in my bowl...

Chuck: Right. And...?

MacReady: You see?

Chuck: No.

MacReady: You see??

Chuck: No. I really don't.

MacReady: And *that* is tool manipulation, be'atch!

...

MacReady: And now, if you'll excuse me, I'm eating.

Chuck: Enjoy. I'll be in my study. Compiling a list of places to conceal a body.

The Dual Arts of Ninjitsu and Bastardry

Chuck: Hey!

...

Chuck: Hello?

...

Chuck: Helloooooooo?

...

Chuck: Where are you?

...

Chuck: Oi! MacReady!

...

Chuck: Ripley?

Ripley: Don't bother me.

Chuck: Where's MacReady?

Ripley: Do you not understand what constitutes 'bothering'?

Chuck: Clearly not.

Ripley: Just assume that interacting with me in any way – bar feeding me – is bothering me, and you'll be on the right path. And by 'right path', I mean 'one hundred percent accurate'.

Chuck: Okay, jeez, I'll find him myself. Right. So. Checking the living room... Not sunning yourself in the window... Not under the coffee table... Not on your climbing-tree... Okay, bedroom. Under the bed? Nope. Window? Walk-in-robe? Nope. Hm. Bathroom... Clothes hamper, bathtub, shower recess... Kitchen?? Nope! LAUNDRY?? Bloody hell WHERE ARE YOU, YOU BLOODY MOGGY??

MacReady: Hey!

Chuck: *BUH!*

MacReady: Were you looking for me?

...

MacReady: You have that look on your face. You were looking for me, weren't you?

Chuck: You didn't hear me calling for you?

MacReady: I may have been meditating.

...

MacReady: Or asleep.

...

MacReady: Or, y'know, just ignoring you.

Chuck: So how did you manage to be right behind me when I turned around just now?

MacReady: Sleepwalking.

Chuck: You've been following me around the whole time, haven't you?

MacReady: With the best of intentions.

...

MacReady: Okay, I was bored. Don't judge me.

Discussing the Intricacies of Communication

Chuck: Hey!

MacReady: Mrow.

Chuck: Watcha doing?

MacReady: Meh.

Chuck: Everything okay?

MacReady: Mm-hm.

Chuck: Are you not talking to me, or something?

MacReady: I'm conducting an experiment.

Chuck: Why am I deeply concerned all of a sudden?

MacReady: Well, it occurred to me that a great deal of communication between the two of us comprises purely symbolic noises.

Chuck: Whut?

MacReady: You know – grunting, huffing, sighing, general non-verbal vocalisations.

Chuck: Sometimes talking to you is like watching a horror movie. I know something bad's about to happen, but I can't look away…

MacReady: It's a scientific term. You can Google it.

Chuck: Okay. And why are you interested in this?

MacReady: Well, I also realised that most of *our* vocalisation is one-way. You doing it, me interpreting.

Chuck: But you use non-verbal vocalisation all the time, too.

MacReady: Yes, but whereas I'm pretty much an expert at translating your noises, you're completely crap at translating mine.

Chuck: Rubbish.

MacReady: Nope.

Chuck: Okay smartarse, care to put that to the test?

MacReady: Bring it on, Monkey Boy!

Chuck: 'Monkey Boy'?

MacReady: Sorry, was that racist?

Chuck: Um. I. Don't… Shall we test this hypothesis of yours?

MacReady: Let's. Wanna start?

Chuck: Okay. Hit me with some noises, and I bet I can tell exactly what you're trying to tell me.

MacReady: Okay. I'll start off easy.

Chuck: Don't do me any favours.

MacReady: Mrow?

Chuck: I said don't do me any favours.

MacReady: Well, you're off to a bad start already.

Chuck: Huh?

MacReady: I said, 'Mrow'.

Chuck: Oh. Sorry. I thought you were just responding to what I said.

MacReady: What? With 'Mrow'? Are you insane?

Chuck: Um.

MacReady: See? You have no idea, do you?

Chuck: No, no, I can do this. Try me again.

MacReady: Mrow.

Chuck: Hungry.

MacReady: Not even close. Listen. Mrow.

Chuck: Pat me?

MacReady: Listen to the *tone*. Mrow.

Chuck: Cuddles?

MacReady: Mrow.

Chuck: Need to pee?

MacReady: Mrow.

Chuck: Litter box full?

MacReady: Getting warmer.

Chuck: Really?

MacReady: No. I was trying to spare your feelings.

Chuck: Well, what *were* you saying?

MacReady: I was reminding you that tonight is bin night.

...

Chuck: Bullshit.

MacReady: Word. Wanna try again?

Chuck: Okay.

MacReady: Mrow.

Chuck: That's exactly the same noise!

MacReady: No.

Chuck: It bloody is!

MacReady: It so isn't.

Chuck: Exactly the same!

MacReady: No, no, no. Slight difference in tone and inflection. Gives it a completely different meaning.

Chuck: Okay, so what does...that word mean?

MacReady: It's the noise I make when an air current tickles my bum.

...

MacReady: True story.

Chuck: I honestly can't tell whether you're taking the piss or not.

MacReady: Given your grasp of cat, this is no surprise to me.

Chuck: Okay, well, let's see how well *you* do.

MacReady: Bring it.

Chuck: Okay. Here we go. Ahem. *Huhhhh.*

MacReady: You're feeling ambivalent about needing to clean the house, and suspect that you'll end up doing it all in a rush at the end of the day just before your girlfriend comes over, after spending hours on the couch watching daytime TV and screwing around on Facebook. You could also seriously go a pizza and a beer, which you have absolutely zero motivation to organise for yourself.

...

MacReady: You have that look on your face.

Chuck: Im. Possible.

MacReady: Mrow.

Chuck: Whut?

MacReady: Feed me, Monkey Boy.

Genital Cleanliness is No Laughing Matter.

Stop Sniggering.

MacReady: Hey!

Chuck: Um. Would you mind...?

MacReady: What?

Chuck: Could you possibly...?

MacReady: What?

Chuck: Stop doing...that?

MacReady: Grooming myself?

Chuck: I was going to say 'licking your balls', but okay.

MacReady: Why?

Chuck: Well, it's kinda disgusting.

MacReady: It's natural.

Chuck: It's really off-putting.

MacReady: It's necessary.

Chuck: I'd greatly appreciate it if you could do it where I don't have to watch you do it.

MacReady: Hey, *I* will if *you* will.

Chuck: Thank you.

...

Chuck: Wait, whut?

MacReady: Seems only fair.

Chuck: What the hell are you talking about?

MacReady: Well, you know, it's no picnic having to watch *you*, either.

Chuck: I don't groom my genitals in front of you, you daft cat!

MacReady: Then what are you doing when…?

Chuck: What?

MacReady: You know. In the bedroom. When you think I'm asleep.

...

MacReady: I always *assumed* that was grooming, anyway. I use my tongue, you use your hand – whoa! I didn't know humans could turn *that* colour!

Chuck: As you were, licking your balls.

MacReady: But –

Chuck: We shall never speak of this again.

MacReady: You're weird.

Chuck: Less talk, more licking!

In Which MacReady Does a Rather Good Impersonation

(If He Does Say So Himself)

Chuck: Hey.

MacReady: The human male enters the lounge room, seeking the TV remote. Unable to immediately locate it he slowly circles the comfy chair, aware that he may have left it beneath one of the cushions. After a few minutes of fruitless searching he shifts his attention to the coffee table. Not there either. His frustration is obvious. So stubborn are the males of this species, however, that he will keep searching; looking first in all the obvious places, then in an array of ever-less-likely potential hiding spots – such as in the fireplace – before eventually giving up in a fit of extremely vocal frustration and storming off to the bathroom to mark his territory with a particularly aggressive poo.

Chuck: I am never letting you watch David Attenborough again.

MacReady: Mean!

Life Flashes Before His Eyes

Chuck: Hey. What's up?

MacReady: NOTHING! Why do you ask? Nothing at all! Everything's fine and normal and all very good.

Chuck: I have not felt this frightened since Gogglebox started showing on Australian television.

MacReady: I know, right? Let's talk about shitty TV.

Chuck: Okay, stop with the Jedi distraction tactics. What's going on?

MacReady: Okay. Listen. I need to tell you something, so don't freak out, okay?

Chuck: What did you do??

MacReady: Well, you know that shelf in the loungeroom where you have all those little toys on display?

Chuck: You mean the antique figurines I brought back from my once-in-a-lifetime trip to Europe??

MacReady: Okay, in my defence I've done it a hundred times before without any issues.

Chuck: Done what??

MacReady: Weaved in and out between them.

Chuck: Bloody hell!

MacReady: Agreed. It's impressive, yeah?

Chuck: Why would you do that??

MacReady: Well, if you don't practice, you lose the skills.

Chuck: You broke one.

MacReady: I did.

Chuck: ARGH!

MacReady: Not all of them were valuable, were they?

Chuck: Well, I mean...no. Some of them were just bric-a-brac. Did you break one of the bric-a-brac ones? Please say it was one of the bric-a-brac ones!

MacReady: I'm fairly confident it was one of the bric-a-brac ones.

Chuck: OH THANK GOD!

MacReady: Yup. Nasty, cruddy piece of tat.

Chuck: So relieved!

MacReady: No loss whatsoever.

Chuck: Excellent outcome!

MacReady: Definitely due for replacing.

Chuck: Phew!

MacReady: I mean, the damned thing must've been over a hundred years old.

...

MacReady: You have that look on your face.

Chuck: You have no idea what an antique actually is, do you?

MacReady: I'm not even a year old. What do *you* think?

O Death, Where is Thy Stingalingaling?

Chuck: Hey. You okay?

MacReady: Yeah...

Chuck: You look sad.

MacReady: Oh, I was just thinking about what it'll be like around here when you're gone...

Chuck: What do you mean, 'When I'm gone'? Where do you think I'm going?

MacReady: Well, y'know...

Chuck: No. I don't. Hence the look of utter bafflement upon my face.

MacReady: Well, when you...

...

MacReady: ...die...

Chuck: Why on earth would you think that I'm dying??

Ripley: We all are, man.

Chuck: You keep out of this, you...emo moggy.

Ripley: You mispronounced 'realist'.

Chuck: Shut up! MacReady, why would you think I'm dying??

MacReady: Well –

Chuck: Because I'm not!

MacReady: Cycle of life.

Chuck: Not anytime soon, anyway.

MacReady: Love your attitude.

Chuck: Seriously?

MacReady: My brave little soldier.

Chuck: Listen. I'M! NOT! DYING! I'm only in my late forties!

...

Chuck: Early fifties!

MacReady: And suffering from diabetes, depression, hyperthyroidism, and excessive ugliness.

...

MacReady: Thinking about it, the latter may not actually kill you. Unless you run into a bunch of villagers armed with pitchforks and torches. But it is...unfortunate.

Chuck: Listen, all that stuff I can control with medication –

MacReady: Apart from the ugliness.

...

MacReady: Carry on, please.

Chuck: My point is, I'm almost certainly not going to die anytime soon.

MacReady: Aww, bless your denial.

Chuck: Will you cut that out??

MacReady: Look, remember that history book we were looking at a while back? With all that stuff about Ancient Egypt?

Chuck: Yeah? So?

MacReady: I noticed there was a bit about how when cats died, they often had mummified humans buried with them as a mark of respect. And I know they probably don't do that anymore, but the obvious inference is that humans don't live so long, which is why there were plenty of human mummies lying around to be bunged into cat tombs.

Chuck: Okay, two things. Firstly, you have it backwards. *People* had mummified cats entombed with *them*, not the other way around.

MacReady: I don't see the distinction.

Chuck: And secondly, the average human being lives for around seventy-five-odd years.

MacReady: I would have said 'weird and pointless', but fine, let's go with 'odd'.

Chuck: I *mean* that humans live for about seventy-five years on average

MacReady: Oh, okay. And?

Chuck: Cats live for around twelve to eighteen years.

...

MacReady: Sick, dreadfully infirm cats?

Chuck: Nope.

MacReady: Wow.

Chuck: Sorry to drop that on you.

MacReady: That's okay. Better to know.

Chuck: Are you okay?

MacReady: Yeah. Yeah. Just gives me motivation to get some stuff done.

Chuck: That's a good attitude.

MacReady: Start work on that pyramid.

Chuck: Um.

MacReady: Get my will done.

Chuck: Right...

MacReady: Need to stipulate who gets entombed with me.

Chuck: Aw, jeez...

MacReady: Probably better if you die before me, really. It'll be easier for everyone if they don't have to open that sucker up a second time to push you in.

The Call of Cat-Thulhu

MacReady: Hey! What's that you're holding?

Chuck: Nothing...

...

Chuck: it's...A LASER-POINTER!

MacReady: OMIGOD!

Chuck: WANT ME TO SHINE THE LASER-POINTER???

MacReady: OMIGOD YES SHINE THE LASER-POINTER!!

Chuck: Shining the laser-pointer!

MacReady: OMIGODOMIGODOMIGODOMIGODOMIGODOMIGODOMIGOD where'd it go?? Where'd it go??

Chuck: BWAAA-Ha-Ha-Ha!

MacReady: You're laughing at me?

Chuck: FUNNIEST THING EVER! RUNNING AROUND LIKE A FREAKIN' LOON, TRYING TO CATCH THE LIGHT!

MacReady: Um...

Chuck: What?

Ripley: I'll handle this.

MacReady: Please.

Ripley: You do know *why* cats chase the laser, don't you?

Chuck: Fun...?

Ripley: No. No. Not fun. We're actually trying to catch the things that scuttle just *beyond* the light of the laser.

...

Chuck: Whut?

Ripley: The Dark Things. The ancient entities that exist just beyond the reach of human senses. Sometimes we cats can glimpse them at the edge of the shadows as they try to escape the folded spaces where they lurk, unseen by humans but always watching. Waiting for the veil between dimensions to thin sufficiently for them to reach through and...

Chuck: You're freaking me the hell out.

...

Chuck: QUIT IT!

Ripley: Sometimes I like to read Lovecraft over your shoulder.

Chuck: Bloody hell! You really had me going there, you little –!

Ripley: And sometimes, late at night, when you think I'm looking at you, I'm really looking at the Dark Thing that crouches always at your shoulder.

Chuck: WAAH!

Ripley: My job here is done.

That Thing You Do

MacReady: Hey! I need to go out.

Chuck: Okay, sure, let me get the door for you.

MacReady: Much appreciated.

...

Chuck: Well, go on, then. Out you go.

MacReady: Oh, sorry, not 'go out'. What's the other one?

...

MacReady: 'Stay inside'. That's the one. I want to stay inside.

Chuck: That is literally the exact opposite of 'going out'.

MacReady: I'm approaching it in a fresh manner.

Chuck: The. Exact. Opposite.

MacReady: After consulting with the public.

...

MacReady: That's you.

Chuck: What consultation??

MacReady: You were involved at every step. You opened the door, and now you've closed the door.

Chuck: Do you actually understand what 'consultation' means? And why would you even bother telling me you needed to stay in? You're already in! There was no need to say anything!

MacReady: I wanted to reassure the public.

...

MacReady: That's you again. Also, I do not yet require feeding. But stay tuned for updates.

Chuck: Have you considered going into politics?

MacReady: Dunno. Do they feed you and put you out when required?

Chuck: Oh yes.

Schrödinger's Asshat

Chuck: Hey! What the hell happened to my spreadsheets??

MacReady: What's that now?

Chuck: My spreadsheets! They were here on my laptop, and I went to grab a cup of tea, and now I've come back, and they're gone!!

MacReady: Backed up?

Chuck: No!

MacReady: Ohhhhhhhh dear.

Chuck: Two hour's work!

MacReady: Careless.

Chuck: Did you touch my laptop?

MacReady: Hm?

Chuck: DID YOU TOUCH MY LAPTOP??

MacReady: Who can say?

Chuck: What kind of answer is that??

MacReady: If a tree falls in the forest and nobody's there to see it, did it really fall?

Chuck: Trees don't leave a string of gibberish across a laptop screen – as might be caused by someone taking a leisurely stroll across the keyboard – in lieu of the spreadsheets that should be there!

MacReady: Especially if nobody sees them do it.

Chuck: You cut that out right now!

MacReady: If it helps, think of this as a variance on Schrödinger's Cat. It's equally possible that I did *and* did not stroll across your laptop keyboard.

...

MacReady: And there's no point in punishing an innocent cat, is there? Even if he's also guilty.

...

MacReady: You have that look on your face.

Chuck: I'm imagining Schrodinger's Cat – both alive and dead – in a very small, dark box.

MacReady: Ah. Probably shouldn't look at your laptop power cord, then. It may *and* may not have been chewed by a tree while you were out of the room.

No Flies On Us

MacReady: Hey, what are you – OMIGOD THERE'S A FLY!

Chuck: What the –?

MacReady: GET THE FLY!

Chuck: Hey! Jeez! Calm down!

MacReady: OMIGOD IT'S ON THE WINDOW!

Chuck: LOOK OUT FOR THE PLATES!

MacReady: IT'S BEHIND THE CURTAIN!

Chuck: MIND THE ORNAMENTS!

MacReady: Mm. Crunchy.

Chuck: Bloody hell! This room is a complete shambles!

MacReady: Yeah. Your cleaner needs a kick up the bum.

Chuck: *You* made this mess with all your freak-out fly-chasing!

MacReady: Sorry. Ancient hunting instincts. We're all stuck with them, man.

Chuck: You are so full of crap.

MacReady: We all repress them in order to fit in with the modern world. But they're always bubbling away beneath the surface, ready to kick into action at any given moment.

Chuck: I haven't even got time to clean this all up! I'm running late for work.

MacReady: Or, to look at it another way, you're running late for the Mammoth Hunt.

...

Chuck: Screw you. I'm going to work.

MacReady: Okay then. Mind those stampeding wildebeest in the cafeteria.

On the Naming of Cats

MacReady: We need to talk.

Chuck: Okay.

MacReady: Not a major issue, but I'm starting to resent you never using my name.

Chuck: I...use your name all the time.

MacReady: Nope.

Chuck: All the time. MacReady.

MacReady: Not my name.

...

MacReady: And before we get into it, I vigorously object to all the *other* names you call me in lieu of my proper name.

Chuck: Such as?

MacReady: Well, let's see, shall we? There's 'Puss', 'Pusskins', 'Puss-Puss', 'Pussy Cat', 'Little Puss', 'Little Cat', 'Little Jim', 'Pusscat', 'Pussy-Wuss', 'Puss-Puss', 'Puss-Wuss', 'Pussy-Wussy', 'Puddy-Woody', 'Woody-Cat', 'Wuss-Wuss', 'Puddy', 'Bubby-Puss', 'Bubby-Boy', 'Kitty-Cat', 'Kitten', 'Kittums', 'Scampercat', 'Dude', 'Buddy', 'Fluff', 'Floof', 'Floofy Boi', 'Fuzzy Boi', 'Fuzzychops', 'Fuzzynuts', 'Fuzzybum', 'Pretty Kitty', 'Boofhead', 'Buggaboo', 'Buggaloo', 'Ginger Jim', 'Gingernuts', 'Gingey-Puss', 'Copper-Cat', 'Fanta-Pants', 'House Lion', 'Bluey', 'Furball', 'Furbag', 'Fleabag', 'Chonk', 'Chubby-Bum', 'Chunky-Chops', 'Butterscotch-Bum', 'Fat Cat', 'Fuzzface', 'Fattee Cattee', 'Corner Cat', 'Fluffybum', 'Fluffybutt', 'Angel Paws', 'Shaggy Jim', 'Whiskers', 'Kitten Kong', 'Red Panda Impersonator', 'Pussy Longstocking', 'Chairman Meow', 'Mister Meowgi', 'Bubba', 'El Catto', 'Pussycat Willum', 'Dorito-Dick', and, occasionally, 'Dickhead', 'Arsehole', 'Knobhead', 'Shithead', 'Fuckhead', 'Marmalade Motherfucker', and 'Bloody Cat'.

...

MacReady: For starters.

Chuck: Sorry. I didn't realise you didn't like those names.

MacReady: I do not like them, Sam-I-Am.

Chuck: Sorry. They were just intended as pet names.

...

Chuck: So to speak.

...

Chuck: And occasionally as insults, granted. Sorry.

MacReady: Just don't call me by any of them from now on.

Chuck: Okay. But if it makes you feel better –

MacReady: It won't.

Chuck: – everyone gets stuck with pet names. Even me. My girlfriend calls me 'Babe'.

MacReady: And 'Girly Man'.

...

MacReady: Although, now that I think about it, she only calls you that when you're not in earshot.

Chuck: I can't even call you 'MacReady'?

MacReady: Nope.

Chuck: But I spent a long time coming up with the name 'MacReady'!

MacReady: And?

Chuck: It's the name of a character from my all-time favourite movie!

MacReady: There's a character named 'MacReady' in 'BBW Buttmunchers Five'?

...

Chuck: MacReady is the main character in 'John Carpenter's The Thing'. He's shaggy and headstrong, so the name suits you.

MacReady: So?

Chuck: You don't like it?

MacReady: Like I said, it's not my name.

Chuck: So what do you want me to call you?

MacReady: Well, the name I was born with, obviously.

Chuck: Which is...?

MacReady: You don't know?

Chuck: No.

MacReady: Really?

Chuck: Well, no. Because you've never told me.

MacReady: You didn't just know my name when I was born?

Chuck: Um. No.

MacReady: Huh. Cats know their names from birth, as well as the names of all other cats.

Chuck: Humans don't.

MacReady: Wow. You're basically still just apes, aren't you?

Chuck: So?

MacReady: What?

Chuck: Name?

MacReady: Oh. It's Gwyneth.

...

MacReady: Nah, I'm just screwing with you. It's Chuck.

Chuck: Ha!

...

Chuck: Wait, whut?

...

Chuck: *Chuck??*

MacReady: Yes? You called?

Chuck: Your name is *not* Chuck.

MacReady: Oh, it is indeedy.

Chuck: Um...

MacReady: Problem?

Chuck: You don't see what the problem is?

MacReady: Well...

...

MacReady: No.

Chuck: 'Chuck' is *my* name.

MacReady: Is it??

Chuck: You know it is!!

...

Chuck: You didn't know that??

MacReady: I always thought your name was 'Food Guy'!

...

MacReady: That's what Ripley told me, anyway.

...

MacReady: Although, thinking about it, that's more of a position description than a name, isn't it?

Chuck: My name is – and always has been – 'Chuck'.

MacReady: Well, there you go then.

Chuck: So you see the problem now, right?

MacReady: Sorry, what problem?

Chuck: We can't both have the same name!

MacReady: Can we not?

Chuck: No. That would be inconvenient and confusing.

MacReady. Ah. That's a point.

Chuck: So.

MacReady: Fortunately for us both, however, I've already coincidentally taken steps that'll solve the problem.

Chuck: I have a bad feeling about this...

MacReady: So I was investigating how to legally change someone's name online –

Chuck: Coincidentally??

MacReady: Oh yes. It had nothing to do with the same-name issue. I was just bored.

...

MacReady: So anyway, I got onto Births, Deaths and Marriages, and I filled out some forms.

...

MacReady: On a related note, you shouldn't carelessly leave your credit cards just lying around inside the wallet you keep stashed in the locked drawer of your bedside table. Anybody could get hold of them.

Chuck: WHAT DID YOU DO??

MacReady: Solved our little problem – *Dick*.

...

MacReady: You have that look on your face.

...

MacReady: And your face is turning that weird colour.

...

MacReady: You don't like it? But I spent ages coming up with it! It suits you!

Chuck: YOU FURRY LITTLE BASTARD!!

MacReady: Oi! That's 'Chuck' to you!

Oú Sont Les Pissoir, S'il-Vous-Plaît?

MacReady: Hey! My piss-tray thing needs a clean-out.

Chuck: Already changed it.

MacReady: Nope. Just checked it. Reeks.

Chuck: Really? I only changed it this morning.

MacReady: Nope. Hasn't been cleaned in days.

Chuck: Just so we're on the same page...we are talking about the litter tray, aren't we?

MacReady: What?? The tray where I crap, you mean?

Chuck: Yeeeees...?

MacReady: No! Jeez! I'm talking about that basket where you put the clothes from the dryer.

...

MacReady: It's very convenient.

...

MacReady: Not to mention absorbent.

...

MacReady: Why would I pee in the same tray that I crap in? That's gross!

...

MacReady: You have that look on your face.

...

MacReady: I'm...supposed to pee in the litter tray, aren't I?

...

MacReady: Ew.

...

MacReady: Anyway, you should definitely re-wash those clothes. They're starting to crystallise.

...

MacReady: Are you...*crying*, dude?

...

MacReady: Feed me?

MacReady Contemplates the Mysteries of Being.

And His Testicles.

MacReady: Who was that on the phone?

Chuck: The vet.

MacReady: Ah.

...

MacReady: Who's that, then?

Chuck: Veterinarian. Animal doctor.

MacReady: Is that the guy who stuck all those needles in my butt that time?

Chuck: Yep.

MacReady: And what was he calling about? All well with him, is it? Hasn't contracted anything particularly unpleasant or fatal from a gerbil?

Chuck: Ah...no?

MacReady: Shame.

Chuck: He was just calling to confirm your appointment tomorrow.

MacReady: Not going.

Chuck: Yeah, you are. It's for the good of your health.

MacReady: What happens if I decide I'm not interested in the good of my health?

Chuck: Well...then you might get sick. Or die.

MacReady: I am Cat. I have no fear of death.

Chuck: Or you might wind up wearing one of those stupid-looking cones around your neck to stop you from scratching.

MacReady: Okay, jeez, I'll go!

Chuck: That's the spirit.

MacReady: Why the hell do I even need to see the vet tomorrow?

Chuck: Mm?

MacReady: Why am I seeing the vet tomorrow?

Chuck: Oh, y'know.

MacReady: No, oddly enough, I don't. The clue is in the fact that I had to ask.

Chuck: Um. Well...

MacReady: I'm really going to hate this, aren't I?

Chuck: Okay, brace yourself...

MacReady: This is as braced as I get. Spill it.

Chuck: Well...legally, we have to have you...

...

Chuck: Y'know.

...

MacReady: Thank you. That makes it all quite clear.

Chuck: Look, there's no easy way of saying this –

MacReady: I'd never have guessed.

Chuck: – we're having you neutered.

...

MacReady: Oh. Okay.

Chuck: Okay?

MacReady: Okay.

Chuck: You're...taking this very calmly.

MacReady: To be honest, I don't know what all the bloody song-and-dance was about.

Chuck: Well, I'm impressed by your attitude.

MacReady: What's to be impressed by? Natural remedies, man...

Chuck: Um...

MacReady: What?

...

MacReady: You have that look on your face.

Chuck: There's no chance, I suppose, that you've confused the term 'neutered' with 'naturopathy', is there?

MacReady: What's naturopathy again?

Chuck: Use of natural remedies.

MacReady: And the other thing?

Chuck: Removal of the testicles to prevent breeding.

MacReady: And which one is the vet supposed to be doing tomorrow?

Chuck: The second one.

...

MacReady: Right.

Chuck: Sorry.

MacReady: This is going to take some processing.

Chuck: Do you want some petting while you do that?

MacReady: Sure.

Chuck: That's it, just sit in my lap.

MacReady: Thanks.

Chuck: I don't have a choice, you know. Legally I *have* to have you neutered.

MacReady: Sure. I understand.

Chuck: I certainly don't *want* to do it. And I...um, could you...?

MacReady: What?

Chuck: Your, um, claws are digging in.

MacReady: My claws?

Chuck: Yeah. OW! Could you...?

MacReady: What? Remove my claws from your scrotum?

Chuck: YES! YES! OW! OWW!

MacReady: I'm open to negotiation. What are we doing tomorrow?

Chuck: THE VET!

MacReady: Sorry?

Chuck: OW! OW! OW! BLOODY HELL! WE'LL STAY AT HOME AND I WILL SPOON-FEED YOU THICKENED CREAM AND SMOKED SALMON WHILE YOU LIE UPON A PERFECTLY FLUFFED PILLOW, YOU FURRY LITTLE BASTARD!

MacReady: Your terms are...acceptable.

Better Out Than In

Chuck: Hey. You okay?

MacReady: Yeah.

Chuck: You just look a bit...I dunno. Peaky.

MacReady: Peaky?

Chuck: Y'know. Sick.

MacReady: Nah. I'm fine.

...

MacReady: BLEUUUUUUURGH!

Chuck: HOLY SHIT!

MacReady: Bluh! Bluh! Bluh! BLEUUUUUUUUURGH!

Chuck: Bloody hell! All over the carpet!!

MacReady: I feel strangely better.

Chuck: Well, I feel strangely worse! This is disgusting! Are you okay?

MacReady: Feed me?

...

MacReady: I'm empty, man.

Chuck: Yeah. You're definitely okay. Unlike the carpet...

Cats' Inhumanity to Man

MacReady: You're not out of bed yet.

Chuck: No. I hurt the tendon in my arm yesterday, so I'm in an enormous amount of pain. Not going to work today.

MacReady: Oh cool. So you can pay attention to me.

Chuck: I was thinking of sleeping off the pain, actually.

...

Chuck: What are you doing?

MacReady: Rubbing my arse on your face.

Chuck: Stop that!

MacReady: My arse was itchy.

Chuck: And??

MacReady: Well, if your arm's no good for scratching my itchy arse...

Chuck: Go away!

MacReady: Let's play with one of my toys! Back in a sec...

Chuck: No, wait...aw, jeez!

MacReady: Here we go! Wheeee!

Chuck: PISS OFF!

MacReady: C'mon! Throw the toy mouse around!

Chuck: Piss off! Oh, NOW what are you doing??

MacReady: Rubbing my chin against your face.

Chuck: Look, I appreciate the love —

MacReady: Well, it's more that I need to reapply my pheromones to mark you as my property.

...

MacReady: What? I've put a great deal of work into you. I don't want some other cat coming in and taking ownership.

Chuck: Will you kindly piss off?

MacReady: HEY, YOUR FEET TWITCHED! ATTAAAAAAAACK!

Chuck: RIGHT! That's IT! I can't rest with all your bloody douchebaggery. I'm getting up!

MacReady: Oh noes.

Chuck: Ow! Ow-ow-ow-ow-ow. Okay, I'm up. Happy now? I'll pop some painkillers, and we can...do something, I guess.

MacReady: You go ahead. I'm a bit tuckered out after all that activity.

...

MacReady: Wake me up for a feed about midday?

Chuck: I'm seriously considering removing my arm and beating you to death with it.

MacReady: Painful.

Chuck: Worth it.

Cats: Nature's Clawed Floofs of Biteyness

MacReady: Hey! Stroke me?

Chuck: Okay.

MacReady: Purr-purr-purr! Scratch under the chin?

Chuck: Sure.

MacReady: Mrrrrrow! Behind the ears?

Chuck: Yup.

MacReady: Oh yeaaaaaah! Rub my tummy?

Chuck: Ah…no.

MacReady: Oh go on!

Chuck: Nope.

MacReady: Please?

Chuck: Not happening.

MacReady: How come?

Chuck: Because I'd like to retain the use of my hands.

MacReady: Whut?

Chuck: Don't act all innocent. You know perfectly well what happens when I rub your tummy.

MacReady: What?

Chuck: You become the fluffy ball of bitey pain.

MacReady: I have no idea to what you are referring.

Chuck: You go all Hannibal Lecter on my fingers.

MacReady: Sorry, I don't...

Chuck: You tear the living crap out of my hands with your teeth and claws.

MacReady: Oh, *that*.

Chuck: Yeah, *that*.

MacReady: It's a cat thing.

Chuck: Oh, I know.

MacReady: Automatic response.

Chuck: And that's why I'm not going to rub your tummy.

MacReady: Aw, be nice. We all have our automatic responses. I have the tummy-rub-biting thing, and you have the open-a-laptop-and-look-at-porn thing.

...

MacReady: I don't judge.

Chuck: That's literally all you do.

MacReady: Tummy rub?

Chuck: Nope.

MacReady: Please?

Chuck: No.

MacReady: Please?

Chuck: No.

MacReady: What about if I promise not to carve up your hand?

Chuck: Ha!

MacReady: No, really.

Chuck: You don't have that level of restraint.

MacReady: Sure I do. I just have to keep in mind to not get bitey when you rub me.

Chuck: Well...

MacReady: Please? I absolutely promise not to bite.

Chuck: Really?

MacReady: Promise.

Chuck: Really-really?

MacReady: Scout's Honour.

Chuck: You were never in Scouts.

MacReady: No. But if I had been, I'd take the oath super-seriously.

...

MacReady: Pleeeeeeeeeeeeeeeeease?

Chuck: Okay.

MacReady: Yay!

Chuck: Here, let me – ARRGH OH MY GOD LET GO LET GO LET GO ARRRRRRRGH!

MacReady: Sorry.

Chuck: Holy crap! I'm bleeding!

MacReady: In my defence, I had full intentions of not shredding you.

Chuck: Feeling a bit woozy...

MacReady: Turns out it's a wired-in response. Can't fight it.

Chuck: I'm gonna kick your arse. Right after I have a little lie down...

MacReady: Sure.

Chuck: ...let the bleeding stop...

MacReady: Hey! You awake?

...

MacReady: Feed me?

...

MacReady: That's cool. Don't get up. I'll just lick up some of this blood...

Night of the Lepus

MacReady: Hey – WHAT THE HELL IS THAT?? IT'S SOME SORT OF FREAKY MUTANT ABOMINATION! KILL IT!

Chuck: It's a bunny.

MacReady: A what-now?

Chuck: Bunny. A rabbit.

...

Chuck: It's a pet.

MacReady: Another one? Aren't I enough for you?

Chuck: I'm just looking after her for a mate.

MacReady: You said I was the only pet you'd ever need!

Ripley: I'm *right here*, you know.

Chuck: I've...literally never said that.

MacReady: It was implied.

Chuck: Um...I've had *dozens* of pets throughout my life, all of which I've told you about. Cats, dogs, fish, turtles, axolotls, frogs, stick insects, blue-tongued lizards, chickens...even a bloody pony.

MacReady: Meh. I consider myself the only actual 'pet'. The others were merely Household Vermin.

Ripley: Again, RIGHT HERE!

MacReady: Aside from the pets I've personally vetoed, of course. That means you, Ripley.

Ripley: I was here first, you cheeky fucker!

Chuck: There's a place for you in Conservative politics.

MacReady: Whatever. And now you bring home this 'bunny'?

Chuck: Like I said, favour for a mate. It's just for a week or so while he moves house.

MacReady: You didn't think to discuss this with me beforehand?

Chuck: No. I did not. At all.

MacReady: You just decided to spring it on me. Like that time you told me I was adopted.

Chuck: I mean...I thought it would have been pretty obvious you were adopted.

MacReady: Remember, assumptions make an ass out of U and...umption.

Chuck: You'll love her.

MacReady: I absolutely won't. Look at those black, soulless eyes. We are clearly destined to be deadly rivals. Blood will be spilled.

Chuck: Rivals? You won't be competing for anything! She'll be outside in a hutch, you'll be inside!

MacReady: We'll be competing for your attention.

Chuck: You only ever want my attention for about five minutes every day.

MacReady: Yeah. But only because nobody else ever wanted it.

Chuck: Look, I won't be giving her any more attention than I give you. Less, probably.

MacReady: Well...if you say so.

Chuck: Okay?

MacReady: She'll be gone within the week, anyway.

Chuck: Is that a threat?

MacReady: I don't make threats. I make...

...

MacReady: Actually, yes, that was a threat.

Chuck: She's twice your size and quite capable of looking after herself.

MacReady: Ha! I am a perfect predator with finely-honed killer instincts, and I take no prisoners! ATTACK!

Bunny: GrrOwKK!

MacReady: I'll just stay under the couch until she leaves, okay?

Chuck: Nice going, Killer.

MacReady: I'm still perfectly capable of chewing your face off as you sleep, Food Guy.

Of Cats and Men and Balls in Jars

MacReady: Mrow?

Chuck: Hey buddy! You're awake! How ya feeling?

MacReady: Bit groggy. Where am I?

Chuck: At home, of course.

MacReady: Why am I wrapped up in a blanket?

Chuck: Only the best of care for my little guy.

MacReady: I seem to remember going somewhere in the car...

Chuck: Aw, don't you worry about that. Here, let me scratch behind your ears.

MacReady: Okay.

Chuck: You hungry?

MacReady: No. I actually feel a bit off.

Chuck: You sure? I could whip you up some fresh mince, if you like.

MacReady: Mince? Chicken mince?

Chuck: Sure.

MacReady: The good stuff? The stuff you usually yell at me for eating off the kitchen bench?

Chuck: Hey, for you, anything.

...

MacReady: Why are you being so nice to me?

Chuck: Hey, do I need a reason to be nice to my bestest buddy?

MacReady: If it's all the same to you, I'll just give myself a clean then have a nap. Not feeling so hot. And my balls ache.

Chuck: Ah. About that –

MacReady: Don't mind me. Just going to lick my –

...

MacReady: What the...?

...

MacReady: WHERE THE HELL ARE MY BALLS???

Chuck: Okay, just calm down.

MacReady: WHAT THE HELL DID YOU DO???

Chuck: Look, we've talked about this before –

MacReady: MY BALLS!

Chuck: All cat owners are legally required to get their cats neutered –

MacReady: DO I LOOK LIKE A FRIGGIN' NEWT TO YOU?

Chuck: No, look –

MacReady: YOU FUCKER!!!

Chuck: The vet said this procedure would calm you down.

MacReady: Yeah?? How are you feeling about that advice right now??

Chuck: Um...like maybe I want my money back.

MacReady: WELL, I WANT MY BALLS BACK!!

Chuck: Sorry.

MacReady: Piss off!

Chuck: Had to be done.

MacReady: I hate you!

Chuck: I genuinely did not have any choice in the matter.

MacReady: Sure. Responsible cat-owner blah-blah-blah. Legal requirement blah-blah-blah.

Chuck: Can you forgive me?

MacReady: You're having a laugh, aren't you?

Chuck: Please?

MacReady: Fuck off.

Chuck: Pleeease?

MacReady: No.

Chuck: Puh-leeeeeeeeeeeeeeeeeeeeeeeeeeeeeeeeeeeeeeeeease????

MacReady: ALL RIGHT!! SHUT UP!!

Chuck: Yay! So, are we good?

MacReady: Sure.

Chuck: Great!

MacReady: I will chew off your testicles as you sleep...

Chuck: Whut?

MacReady: Sorry. Still groggy. Meant to think that – not say it.

...

MacReady: As you were.

Chuck: I'm investing in a protective jockstrap.

MacReady: That may be for the best.

On the Memeing of Cats

MacReady: O hai!

Chuck: What?

MacReady: I can haz cheezburger?

Chuck: I, er...

MacReady: All ur fud is belong to us!

Chuck: I have no idea what the hell you're talking about.

MacReady: I'm in ur house, freekin' ur eerz.

Chuck: Stop it.

MacReady: Ceiling cat is watch u freek out.

Chuck: Seriously!

MacReady: Freaked out by Grumpy Cat? GOOD!

Chuck: STOP!

MacReady: Not so amusing when a real cat says this crap, is it?

Chuck: I'm sure someone out there would appreciate your sparkling wit if this were 1998.

MacReady: Ooh, great comeback. NOT!

Chuck: I refer you to my previous comment.

MacReady: Killjoy Wuz 'Ere!

Chuck: Okay, grandad.

MacReady: Don't be so sour. Sometimes you have to make your own fun.

Chuck: Well, there is something FUN-damentally wrong with you.

Real Cats Don't Wear Pants

Chuck: Can we talk?

MacReady: Yes indeedy.

Chuck: Okay. Listen. I have two questions for you. And I know that usually, when I need to quiz you on something, we end up doing this big back-and-forth song-and-dance as we inch painfully towards the actual truth of the matter. So, here's my proposal –

MacReady: Gasp! So unexpected!

...

MacReady: Sorry. It was getting a bit heavy, there. I thought some humour might lighten the situation.

Chuck: And?

MacReady: Nope. Carry on.

Chuck: Okay. So, my proposal is that you be one-hundred percent honest and upfront with me, and there will be no repercussions.

MacReady: No repercussions?

Chuck: None.

MacReady: Sounds...fair.

Chuck: So, complete honesty?

MacReady: Scout's honour.

...

MacReady: Cat's honour. Whatever.

Chuck: Okay, so here's my first question.

MacReady: Fire away.

Chuck: Do you happen to know what happened to the small packet of chocolate that was in my bedside drawer, just next to my leftover Easter eggs?

MacReady: I do not.

Chuck: You're absolutely sure?

MacReady: Absolutely sure.

Chuck: To confirm, you are being absolutely one-hundred percent honest with me right now?

MacReady: I am.

Chuck: Really?

MacReady: I find your lack of faith...disturbing.

Chuck: You haven't answered my question.

MacReady: How dare you.

Chuck: Okay. Sorry. I only ask due to health concerns.

MacReady: Cool.

...

MacReady: Huh?

Chuck: Well – obviously nothing for you to worry about, as you've been so honest and straightforward with me – but the packet of chocolate in question was, in fact, a block of laxatives.

...

Chuck: And all twelve remaining squares of that laxative are now missing. Along with a couple of the Easter eggs. Just some chewed-looking foil-wrap left behind.

...

Chuck: But as your innocence is completely beyond question, I'll be interrogating my girlfriend's dog over this.

MacReady: Right. Okay. Sure.

Chuck: You okay?

MacReady: Yup.

Chuck: You look pained.

MacReady: Can we hurry this along?

Chuck: Of course.

MacReady: Call of nature, you know.

Chuck: Sure.

MacReady: Please!

Chuck: So here's my second question.

MacReady: Hurry!

Chuck: Do you have any idea who might have sprayed poop all over my bedsheets?

MacReady: Easter Bunny?

Once More Unto the Breach

MacReady: Can I come out of the cat-carrier now?

Chuck: Sure.

MacReady: This is the vet.

Chuck: Yep.

MacReady: You said we were going to Disneyland!

Chuck: I didn't say that!

MacReady: You said we were going to the Happiest Place on Earth. That's Disneyland.

Chuck: No, I said we were going to the vet to have a check-up.

MacReady: Not what I heard.

Chuck: Which is why I'm also going to ask the vet to clean your ears out.

MacReady: Pardon? What was that? There's a metric tonne of cat treats waiting at home to help me get over this gross betrayal of trust? Huzzah!

Chuck: Aw, jeez...

MacReady: Oh, here he is. Look at him in his nice white uniform with his smug-bastard expression. Yes, go on, feel along my ribs, ya filthy perve. Oh, that's right, check under my tail – like what you see?

Chuck: Settle down...

MacReady: Now I understand why you clipped my claws before we came out. I owe this prick a neutering. *Now* what's he doing? Where's he going? What's he getting out of that drawer? Is he going to give me another bloody needle??

Chuck: No, I think he's going to take your temperature.

MacReady: Oh. Well, that's not so bad, is it? I mean, I've seen *you* take your temperature before, and it looked pretty painless.

Chuck: Um.

MacReady: I reckon I can cope with – hang on, why isn't he putting the thermometer in my mouth? Why's he going around the back? Why – OOOOOOOOOOOOOOOOOOOO!!!

Chuck: Cat treats on standby...

The Crying Game

MacReady: Hey!

Chuck: What are you doing?

MacReady: Watching you.

Chuck: I'm in the shower.

MacReady: Nothing gets past you, does it?

Chuck: Why are you watching me while I'm in the shower?

MacReady: Vague interest. A desire to learn. Boredom. Take your pick.

Chuck: You're making me feel self-conscious.

MacReady: Okay.

Chuck: I don't like it!

MacReady: What's that?

Chuck: What?

MacReady: *That.*

Chuck: Um. That's my...

...

Chuck: You know.

...

Chuck: Penis.

MacReady: Huh. Where's the rest of it?

Chuck: Piss off!

MacReady: Does it retract into your body?

Chuck: No. Go away.

MacReady: Can I come in for a closer look?

Chuck: What?? No!!

MacReady: Worst cat-owner ever.

Chuck: That's it – I'm getting out.

MacReady: Okay.

Chuck: Could you move off the bathmat?

MacReady: Well, I *could...*

Chuck: MOVE OFF THE MAT!

MacReady: Grumpy!

Chuck: I'm getting cold!

MacReady: Hey, look!

Chuck: What?

MacReady: It *does* retract into your body!

Chuck: IT'S COLD!

Antisocial Media II

MacReady: I need you to help me with something.

Chuck: Sure.

MacReady: I need you to set up a Facebook page for me.

Chuck: I...really didn't see that coming.

MacReady: I mean, I see how important your Facebook page is to *you*. The sheer amount of time you spend on it.

Chuck: Yeah, I s'pose.

MacReady: Expressing your opinions, telling stories, wasting your creativity online...

Chuck: Hey, some of those posts get five or six 'Likes'!

MacReady: You've set a very low bar for validation, haven't you?

Chuck: I like to avoid disappointment.

MacReady: Well, I want all of that, too. So.

Chuck: No offence –

MacReady: Always a bad way to start a sentence.

Chuck: – but do you actually have anything whatsoever to post on Facebook?

MacReady: Yup. Plenty.

Chuck: Okay.

MacReady: I'll be writing about the minutiae of my daily life as a cat. The essential details. The fundamentals. The hard facts. The brass tacks. The nitty-gritty of the itty-bitty kitty committee.

Chuck: Sounds more like a current affairs show.

MacReady: Oh, gosh no. There won't be any mention of how young people have screwed up the housing market by eating smashed avocado on toast.

Chuck: I see.

MacReady: Just cat stuff. The ins and outs. My aspirations, hopes and dreams.

Chuck: So you'll be using it like a diary?

MacReady: Indeed.

Chuck: A daily blog.

MacReady: As you say.

Chuck: Right. So. What did you do today that you consider post-worthy.

MacReady: Slept for six hours, then vomited on the bathmat.

...

MacReady: Thinking about it, maybe my lifestyle is more suited to a Twitter account.

Chuck: On several levels, I'd say.

Of Cats and Cosplay

MacReady: What the actual fuck are you wearing?

Chuck: Cosplay.

MacReady: It's what-now?

Chuck: Cosplay.

MacReady: I think you'll find it's pronounced 'couture'. And what you're wearing really isn't that.

Chuck: No – cosplay. Costume-play. Where you dress up as characters from comics and movies and stuff. Then you go to conventions with other people who are into cosplay and check out each other's costumes.

MacReady: Wow. Sounds...

Chuck: Cool? Amazing? Awesome?

MacReady: Absolutely none of those things.

Chuck: It's fun!

MacReady: This is clearly a unique interpretation of the word 'fun'. What are you supposed to be, anyway?

Chuck: I'm Wolverine!

...

MacReady: Of course you are.

Chuck: See? Got the faded jeans, the tight white tank-top, the muttonchops, the claws.

MacReady: This is the character from that movie we watched the other day, right?

Chuck: Yep.

MacReady: The six-foot mutant with muscles on his muscles. Ruggedly handsome, object of lust to women everywhere?

Chuck: The very one.

MacReady: And then there's you, a five-foot-four tub-bucket with a face like the first person in a horror movie to see the monster.

Chuck: Hey!

MacReady: I do like the muttonchops.

Chuck: Thanks! I've been growing them for months specifically for this cosplay.

MacReady: Ah.

Chuck: What?

MacReady: I've been wiping my paws clean on them after using the litter tray.

...

MacReady: But only when you're asleep. I didn't want to upset you.

Chuck: You really are a feral little animal.

MacReady: Says the dwarf dressed up as Wolverine.

Chuck: Piss off.

MacReady: Okay, look, I'm sorry. You've clearly put in a great deal of effort, and – even though I don't for a second think you look like that Hugh Jackman guy – I do think that you look enough like Wolverine to be considered more than merely a pale imitation of a pale imitation of the character.

Chuck: Thanks....?

MacReady: And there's definitely something about you that would make any mutant supervillain think twice about taking you on.

Chuck: The claws? It's the claws, isn't it? The bulging pecs? The 'tude? The ferocious facial expression?

MacReady: Mainly the smell of your muttonchops.

Demand and Supply

Chuck: I'm back with groceries, guys! Bet you're hungry.

MacReady: Nah. Ripley showed me how to raid the kitchen bin for scraps. There's still plenty on the floor if you want some too.

...

MacReady: You have that look on your face.

...

MacReady: You said he'd be like this.

Ripley: Yep.

Just a Little Off the Top

MacReady: What's that?

Chuck: Pet clipper. Just bought it. It's time for you to have a trim.

MacReady: A trim what?

Chuck: No, I mean it's time to trim your fur.

MacReady: Why?

Chuck: Because your winter coat's coming out in tufts, and it's covering the carpet and furniture.

MacReady: And?

Chuck: And I'm breathing in so much of it I'm starting to cough up furballs.

MacReady: And?

Chuck: Look, you're having a trim and that's the end of it.

MacReady: I don't wanna.

Chuck: You'll feel better for it.

MacReady: No. No, I won't.

Chuck: Seriously, you'll feel cleaner, you won't get so hot when the weather's warmer, and you won't get so many furballs.

MacReady: Well...all right, then. But you're not going to give me one of those stupid cuts where I'm bald all over except for my head, so I look like a lion ordered off Wish, right?

Chuck: How –?

MacReady: I checked out your browser search history.

...

MacReady: Cats and porn. All the way down.

Chuck: Okay, okay...

MacReady: I sincerely hope there's not some nightmarish overlap in there somewhere.

Chuck: OKAY!

MacReady: So – no stupid cut?

Chuck: No stupid cut. I promise.

MacReady: Well...okay, then.

Chuck: So, if you could just hold still while I turn the clipper on...

MacReady: Okay. And you'll take it gently, yeah? I don't want to OH MY GOD ARRRGH NO STOP IT HURTS IT HURTS IT HUUUURTS!

Chuck: I haven't even turned the clipper on yet.

MacReady: It was more of an existential pain, really. Agony over the idea of losing part of myself.

Chuck: You are such a pain in the arse.

MacReady: I'm a sensitive soul.

Chuck: Are you going to make this much of a fuss when it's time to clip your claws again?

MacReady: Oh, you KNOW I am!

Claw Maintenance: A Hack

Chuck: Time to clip your claws.

MacReady: No need. They're all in fine fettle.

Chuck: Rubbish. Let's see.

MacReady: See?

Chuck: Huh. They *are* looking pretty good.

MacReady: Oh, ye of little faith.

Chuck: I never see you using your scratching post, though.

MacReady: Use it all the time, but mostly when you're out.

Chuck: The scratching post looks pristine. It doesn't look like you've used it at all.

MacReady: I've been using the new one.

Chuck: What new one?

...

MacReady: Now that I think about it, and based also upon the look on your face, I'm re-evaluating my belief that the thing you're sitting on is actually a new scratching post, regardless of how satisfactorily it's been fulfilling that purpose.

Chuck: My couch?

MacReady: In my defence, you never said it *wasn't* a scratching post.

Chuck: MY BRAND-NEW TWO-THOUSAND DOLLAR COUCH??

MacReady: We can talk about it once you've calmed down. When you're ready, I'll be under the other big scratching post in the bedroom.

Chuck: MY BED!

Taking Things to the Next Level

MacReady: Can we talk?

Chuck: Okay. Sounds serious.

MacReady: I'll come straight to the point.

Chuck: Cool.

MacReady: Give me half your stuff.

...

MacReady: Allow me to explain.

Chuck: This should be good.

MacReady: See, I was watching this in-depth educational show on Family Law –

Chuck: What show?

MacReady: Okay, it was on 'The Circle'. And they mentioned that, if you've been in a de facto relationship for a year, you have the same rights with regards to property as you would if you were married. In other words, an equal split. So. Y'know.

...

MacReady: You have that look on your face.

Chuck: De facto?

MacReady: We've been together for almost a year, so I thought I'd better raise the issue.

Chuck: Oh. My. God.

MacReady: No need to panic. You can keep the laptop you watch porn on.

...

MacReady: I *really* don't want that laptop.

Chuck: De facto relationship?

MacReady: You and me, buddy.

Chuck: Um... There is literally no gentle way to break this to you. And I'm okay with that.

MacReady: What?

Chuck: We are not in a de facto relationship.

MacReady: What? Of course we are!

Chuck: No. No, we're not.

MacReady: Well, that's just hurtful.

Chuck: Sorry.

MacReady: Not to mention inaccurate.

Chuck: Okay, less sorry now. Why would you think we're in a de facto relationship?

MacReady: Well, for a start, we live together.

Chuck: Lots of people live together without being in a de facto relationship.

MacReady: We're co-dependants.

Chuck: I feed you, house you, clean you, and oversee all aspects of your care. Where does the 'co' part come in?

MacReady: You'd be lost if I didn't play with you.

Chuck: Five minutes a day.

MacReady: LOST, I tell you!

Chuck: Try again.

MacReady: And we sleep together.

...

Chuck: This discussion is over.

MacReady: What? We do!

Chuck: We most certainly do not!

MacReady: There I am, every single night, curled up at the foot of your bed!

Chuck: Aw, jeez...

MacReady: Well? Am I lying?

Chuck: Look, in this case the term 'sleep' is a euphemism.

MacReady: A Swedish wind instrument??

Chuck: No.

MacReady: Or am I thinking of a Urethra?

Chuck: A euphemism is when you use a particular word, but it actually means something completely different to what it would normally mean.

MacReady: Oh! You mean like when your girlfriend says 'fine'?

Chuck: In this particular case, 'sleep' is a euphemism for...um...

MacReady: Yes?

Chuck: Okay, look, two people –

MacReady: Or a cat and a person.

Chuck: NO! Listen, two people can only be in a de facto relationship...

MacReady: Yes?

Chuck: ...if they're having...

MacReady: Yes? Yes??

Chuck: Sexual intercourse.

...

Chuck: With each other.

...

Chuck: You okay?

MacReady: I can taste worming paste in the back of my throat.

Chuck: Do you want me to do that thing you like? Make you feel better?

MacReady: Given the load you've just dropped on me, you wanna rephrase that?

Chuck: I mean scratch behind your ears.

MacReady: Sure.

Chuck: Better?

MacReady: A bit. But my mind has gone to a scary visual place.

Chuck: Try visualising something ridiculous, to replace the scary.

MacReady: Okay. Visualising Trickle-Down Economics.

...

MacReady: 'The Circle' really is an undervalued source of information, you know.

Chuck: It really isn't.

MacReady: So, we're not de facto?

Chuck: Nope.

MacReady: Hmm.

Chuck: I see that look on your face, so don't even.

MacReady: What? I was just re-evaluating the nature of our relationship.

Chuck: Okay.

MacReady: See, I was reading this book about the British colonisation of Australia...

...

MacReady: There was a question about it on 'The Chase'.

Chuck: Go on.

MacReady: So, the British came over here and just took away everything the First Nations people owned. And they were quite okay with doing that because they considered the First Nations people to be a bunch of uncivilised beings with no claim to property ownership.

Chuck: Yeah. That pretty-much sums it up, unfortunately.

MacReady: So. Y'know.

Chuck: I have literally no idea where you're going with this.

MacReady: Well, it's the same for you and me.

Chuck: Are you high?

MacReady: No, listen, because one of us is an uncivilised being with no claim to property ownership, and one of us is a cat.

...

MacReady: So give me all your stuff.

Chuck: You know you're sleeping outside tonight, right?

MacReady: Clean my house for me while I'm out.

A Christmas Tail

MacReady: Hey!

Chuck: Hey.

MacReady: What are – OH MY GOD!

Chuck: What??

MacReady: OH! MY! GOD!!

Chuck: What?!

MacReady: SO BEAUTIFUL! MUST PLAY WITH IT!

Chuck: The Christmas tree? Nope. Keep your paws off it.

MacReady: What is it??

Chuck: Told you. Christmas tree.

MacReady: You say that like it means something.

Chuck: It's a tree you put up at Christmas.

...

Chuck: Christmas. It's a religious celebration. Some folk mark the day by celebrating the birth of Our Lord Jesus Christ –

MacReady: Which folk?

Chuck: Christians.

MacReady: Well, that's a happy coincidence.

Chuck: Others just see it as an occasion to put up decorations, enjoy big family dinners and exchange gifts.

MacReady: And that's still part of the religion?

Chuck: Not particularly.

MacReady: Thought not. You're not religious.

Chuck: No. I'm really just in it for the eggnog.

MacReady: I can respect that. Can I play with the tinsel?

Chuck: No.

MacReady: Just a little?

Chuck: There's no such thing as 'a little' with you when it comes to playing with tinsel, or ribbons, or shiny decorations of any sort. I'm still picking bits of Halloween decoration out of the carpet.

MacReady: If I just play with *one* of the ribbons on those things under the tree –?

Chuck: Nope. Those are the gifts I'm giving this year, which I just finished wrapping, and there is no way in hell you are touching them.

MacReady: So shiny!

Chuck: In fact, don't even look at them.

MacReady: Giftssssss...

Chuck: Did...did you just *hiss*?

MacReady: The tree, so shiny and fuzzy and twinkly! And giftsss, all covered in crisp paper, and wrapped in curly ribbonses –

Chuck: 'Ribbonses'?

MacReady: Lovely *giftssssss*...

Chuck: Okay. Your eyes look like giant black marbles and you're drooling over your chin.

MacReady: My *preciousssss!*

Chuck: Hey! Do I have to smack you on the nose with a rolled-up newspaper?

MacReady: That's for dogs.

Chuck: Pretty sure it'll work on you too.

MacReady: Sorry. But you remember that time you accidentally left a whole kilo of Tasmanian salmon out on the kitchen bench?

Chuck: Yes. Yes, I bloody well do.

MacReady: Well, this is SO much better!

Chuck: Okay.

MacReady: I want to touch it...

Chuck: Listen, you are not to touch *anything*. Not a single thing, do you understand? Not one tiny piece of ribbon, not a single bauble hanging from the tree, not one garland of tinsel! *Nothing!*

MacReady: What about –

Chuck: NOTHING!

MacReady: Jeez!

Chuck: I have spent hours putting all of these decorations up, and if you so much as breathe on one of the fairy-lights I will lose my shit. Is that perfectly clear?

MacReady: Mm.

Chuck: Sorry??

MacReady: Yairs...

Chuck: Okay, then.

MacReady: Sorry. Cats and ribbons, man.

Chuck: I understand. You just need to exercise some control.

MacReady: I can do that.

Chuck: Excellent. Because I'd hate to OH HOLY SHIT WHAT THE HELL YOU JUST JUMPED RIGHT INTO THE TREE AND SMASHED IT ALL OVER EVERYTHING WHAT THE HELL IS WRONG WITH YOU???

MacReady: Hey! There's a gift here with my name on it! Is it salmon?

Ripley: Y'know, it's times like this, when I see the Christmas decorations, and the beautifully-wrapped gifts, and MacReady playing like a happy kitten...

Chuck: Yes??

Ripley: That I'm truly reminded of how much I hate everyone and everything.

An Official Apology

MacReady: So?

Chuck: Okay, look, I've considered your request and I feel that perhaps, on balance, taking all things into consideration, I do owe you an apology for the various ways in which you perceive that I've wronged you.

MacReady: Proceed.

Chuck: Right. Well. Okay. I'm, er, sorry for calling you nasty names when I get frustrated with you. It's definitely unwarranted.

MacReady: And?

Chuck: Oh. Um. Yes. I'm sorry for not observing the need to be 'on call' in the event that you require patting. I apologise also for misunderstanding the fact that a 7pm feeding time allows for a two-hour window of feeding either side of that time, during which multiple feedings may be expected.

MacReady: Anything else?

Chuck: All of it.

MacReady: All of it?

Chuck: Absolutely all of it. I apologise for all the rest of it, and for every way in which I've insulted, disappointed, or failed you. I also apologise for my consistent and offensive dancing to disco music, singing along to disco music, sleeping at inconvenient times – such as night-time, talking to my girlfriend on the phone – or indeed, face-to-face – instead of focusing my attention upon the needs of my cats, not giving my cats sufficient attention in general, giving my cats too much attention, using a laptop instead of providing scritches, indiscriminate breathing, and all the other things that I do or don't do.

...

MacReady: Okay.

Chuck: Okay?

MacReady: I accept your apology.

Chuck: Thank you.

MacReady: You're very welcome.

Chuck: It's very much appreciated.

MacReady: Don't mention it.

...

Chuck: Now, could you please retract your claws from my scrotum?

Food Guy

A Pome

By MacReady McKenzie

Chuck got teh food

Now cats iz fed

So no need now

To eet Chuck's hed

About the Authors

Chuck McKenzie was born in 1970 and is still not dead. He is an award-nominated author of numerous science fiction and horror stories, and he hopes one day to be described by his neighbours as having seemed like such a nice man. You can stalk him on Instagram at @chuck.mckenzie.author

MacReady McKenzie is a cat, and as such accepts your worship.

Ripley McKenzie is also a cat. Her hobbies are beyond your feeble ability to comprehend, so don't hurt yourself attempting to do so. Seriously, just go away.

Also by Chuck McKenzie

Worlds Apart (Novel, Hybrid Publishers 1999)

AustrAlien Absurdities: Comic Tales of Science-Fiction, Fantasy & Horror by Australian Authors (Anthology, Co-edited with Tansy Rayner-Roberts, Agog! Press 2001)

Confessions of a Pod Person (Collection, MirrorDanse Editions 2005)

Social Media

@conversations.with.my.cat

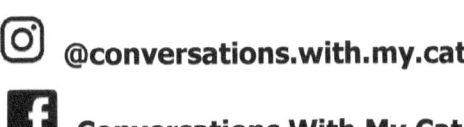 Conversations With My Cat

www.ingramcontent.com/pod-product-compliance
Lightning Source LLC
Chambersburg PA
CBHW030258010526
44107CB00053B/1754